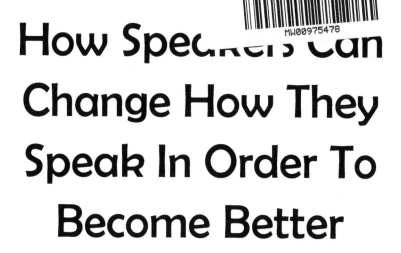

How Speakers Can Change How They Speak In Order To Become Better

Change techniques that will transform a speech into a memorable event

"Practical, proven techniques that will help you to make your next speech a success"

Dr. Jim Anderson

Published by:
Blue Elephant Consulting
Tampa, Florida

Printed in the United States of America

Library of Congress Control Number: 2019903792

ISBN-13: 9781092359610

Warning – Disclaimer

The purpose of this book is to educate and entertain. This book does not promise or guarantee that anyone following the ideas, tips, suggestions, techniques or strategies will be hired. It is the discretion of employers if you will or will not be hired. The author, publisher and distributor(s) shall have neither liability nor responsibility to anyone with respect to any loss or damage caused, or alleged to be caused, directly or indirectly by the information contained in this book.

Recent Books By The Author

Product Management

- Killer Ways To Make Partnerships Work For Product Managers: Techniques For Product Managers To Find Ways To Work With Others In Order To Make Their Product Successful

- How Product Managers Can Sell More Of Their Product: Tips & Techniques For Product Managers To Better Understand How To Sell Their Product

Public Speaking

- Delivering Excellence: How To Give Presentations That Make A Difference: Presentation techniques that will transform a speech into a memorable event

- How To Rehearse In Order To Give The Perfect Speech: How to effectively rehearse your next speech to that your message be remembered forever!

CIO Skills

- What CIOs Need To Know In Order To Successfully Manage An IT Department: Decision Making Skills That Every CIO Needs To Have In Order To Be Able To Make The Right Choices

- How CIOs Can Make Innovation Happen: Tips And Techniques For CIOs To Use In Order To Make Innovation Happen In Their IT Department

IT Manager Skills

- Building The Perfect Team: What Staffing Skills Do IT Managers Need?: Tips And Techniques That IT Managers Can Use In Order To Correctly Staff Their Teams

- Secrets Of Effective Leadership For IT Managers: Tips And Techniques That IT Managers Can Use In Order To Develop Leadership Skills

Negotiating

- Use The Power Of Arguing To Win Your Next Negotiation: How To Develop The Skill Of Effective Arguing In A Negotiation In Order To Get The Best Possible Outcome

- Learn How To Signal In Your Next Negotiation: How To Develop The Skill Of Effective Signaling In A Negotiation In Order To Get The Best Possible Outcome

Miscellaneous

- How To Heal A Broken Leg – Fast!: Understanding how to deal with a broken leg in order to start walking again quickly

- How Software Defined Networking (SDN) Is Going To Change Your World Forever: The Revolution In Network Design And How It Affects

Note: See a complete list of books by Dr. Jim Anderson at the back of this book.

Acknowledgements

Any book like this one is the result of years of real-world work experience. In my over 25 years of working for 7 different firms, I have met countless fantastic people and I've been mentored by some truly exceptional ones. Although I've probably forgotten some of the people who made me the person that I am today, here is my attempt to finally give them the recognition that they so truly deserve:

- Thomas P. Anderson
- Art Puett
- Bobbi Marshall
- Bob Boggs

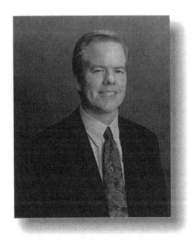

Dr. Jim Anderson

This book is dedicated to my family: Lori, Maddie, Nick, and Ben. None of this would have been possible without their constant love and support.

Thanks for always believing in me and providing me with the strength to always be willing to go out there and be my best for you.

Blue Elephant Consulting
Speaking. Negotiating. Managing. Marketing.

Table Of Contents

TO BECOME BETTER SPEAKERS WE NEED TO KNOW HOW TO CHANGE 9

ABOUT THE AUTHOR 11

CHAPTER 1: HOW TO GIVE A SPEECH WHEN YOU ARE NOT THE ONE DOING THE TALKING 16

CHAPTER 2: HOW PUBLIC SPEAKERS CAN MINIMIZE THEIR ACCENT 21

CHAPTER 3: BOUNCING BACK FROM A REALLY BAD SPEECH 25

CHAPTER 4: LEARN TO READ YOUR NEXT AUDIENCE LIKE A BOOK ...29

CHAPTER 5: HOW TO DEAL WITH SPEAKING ANXIETY WHEN IT COMES 33

CHAPTER 6: EYE SEE WHAT YOU ARE TALKING ABOUT 38

CHAPTER 7: WHAT HAPPENS TO YOUR SPEECH WHEN YOU'RE DONE TALKING? 43

CHAPTER 8: WHAT YOU'VE NEVER BEEN TAUGHT ABOUT BEING A SUCCESSFUL SPEAKER 48

CHAPTER 9: 3 VERY SMALL WAYS TO BECOME A BETTER SPEAKER ..53

CHAPTER 10: HOW TO MAKE YOUR NEXT SPEECH UNFORGETTABLE 57

CHAPTER 11: HOW TO BECOME A SPEAKER WHO IS AN ONLINE LEADER 62

CHAPTER 12: HOW TO GROW YOUR SPEAKING ABILITIES 67

To Become Better Speakers We Need To Know How To Change

Every speaker would like to become a better speaker. After each speech that we give, we all think to ourselves about the things that we could have done differently that would have gotten a better reaction from our audience. The trick is that we have to remember the changes that we need to make and then we need to make them. That's what this book is all about – helping you to remember how you can become a better public speaker.

As speakers we need to keep in mind that we won't always be the one doing the speaking. However, this just requires us to do things a little bit differently. If when we speak we have an accent that is different than that of our audience, we need to take steps to minimize it. Change is the first thing on our minds when we give a speech that turns out badly. The key is knowing what needs to be changed so that won't happen again.

In order to give a good speech, you need to know your audience. You have to be about to understand what they want to get out of your speech. This can cause a speaker to start to feel anxious and when that happens we need to have ways to deal with it. When we finally make it to the end of our speech we might think that we are done with our talk. It turns out that that is not the case – things may be just starting for us.

Every time that we give a speech we all share the same goal. We want our speech to be unforgettable for our audience. This can be done and in fact, if we can find out how to become an online leader, then we may have prepared our audience for a great speech even before we take the stage. Use this book to learn

9

how to grow your speaking abilities and you'll discover that you have become a better speaker.

For more information on what it takes to be a great public speaker, check out my blog, The Accidental Communicator, at:

www.TheAccidentalCommunicator.com

Good luck!

- Dr. Jim Anderson

About The Author

I must confess that I never set out to be a public speaker. When I went to school, I studied Computer Science and thought that I'd get a nice job programming and that would be that. Well, at least part of that plan worked out!

My first job was working for Boeing on their F/A-18 fighter jet program. I spent my days programming fighter jet software in assembly language and I loved it. The U.S. government decided to save some money and went looking for other countries to sell this plane to. This put me into an unfamiliar role: I started to meet with foreign military officials and I ended up having to give speeches in order to explain what my product did.

Time moved on and so did I. I found myself working for Siemens, the big German telecommunications company. They were making phone switches and selling them to the seven U.S. phone companies. The problem was that the switches were too complicated. Customers couldn't tell the difference between one complicated phone switch from another complicated phone switch. Once again I found myself standing in front of the room giving speeches in order to explain what these complicated machines did and why ours were better than anyone else's.

I've spent over 25 years working as a product manager for both big companies and startups. This has given me an opportunity to do many, many presentations for customers, at conferences, and everywhere in-between.

I now live in Tampa Florida where I spend my time managing my consulting business, Blue Elephant Consulting, teaching college courses at the University of South Florida, and traveling to work with companies like yours to share the knowledge that I have about how to create and deliver powerful and effective speeches.

I'm always available to answer questions and I can be reached at:

Dr. Jim Anderson
Blue Elephant Consulting
Email: jim@BlueElephantConsulting.com
Facebook: http://goo.gl/1TVoK
Web: **www.BlueElephantConsulting.com**

"Unforgettable communication skills that will set your ideas free..."

Create Speeches That Motivate Your Audiences And Get Your Message Heard!

Dr. Jim Anderson is available to provide training and coaching on the topics that are the most important to people who have to speak in public: how can I create a speech that people want to hear and how can I deliver in a way that will allow me to connect with my audience and get my point across to them?

Dr. Anderson believes that in order to both learn and remember what he says, speakers need to laugh. Each one of his speeches is full of fun and humor so that what he says "sticks" with everyone.

Dr. Anderson's Public Speaking Training Includes:

1. How to plan your next speech: pick your purpose and understand your audience.
2. What's the best way to get PowerPoint and Keynote to work with you, not against you?
3. What do you need to do when you are presenting in order to truly connect with your audience?

Dr. Jim Anderson presents over 100 speeches per year. To invite Dr. Anderson to speak at your event, contact him at:

Phone: 813-418-6970 or
Email: jim@BlueElephantConsulting.com

Blue
Elephant
Consulting
Speaking.   Negotiating.   Managing.   Market

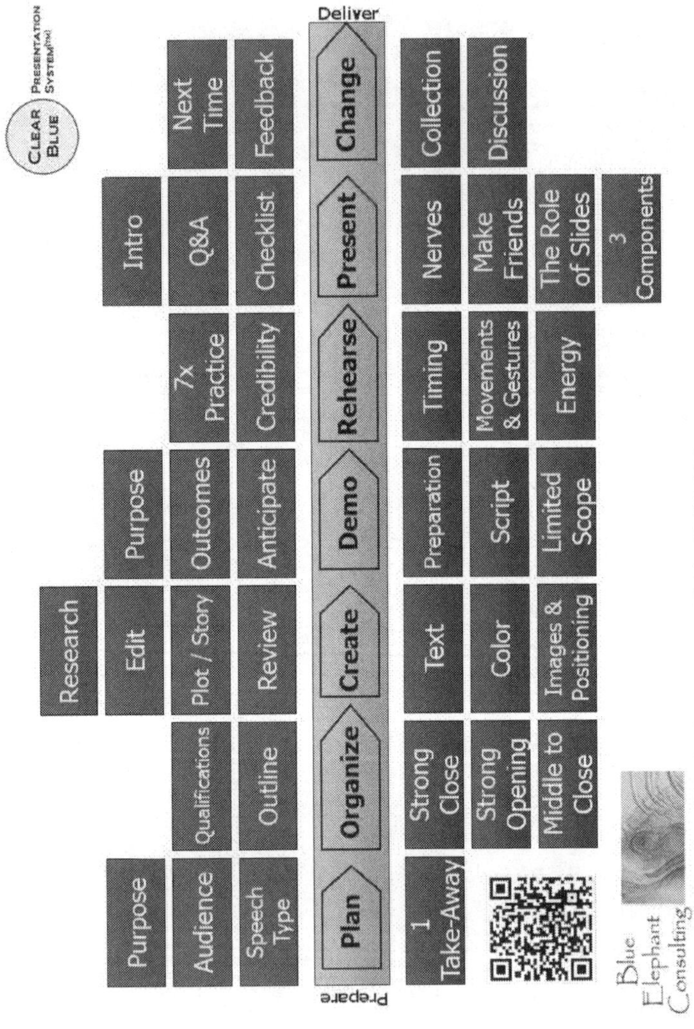

CLEAR BLUE Presentation System™

Deliver: Plan → Organize → Create → Demo → Rehearse → Present → Change

Prepare

Diagram labels:
- Purpose, Audience, Speech Type
- Qualifications, Outline
- Research, Edit, Plot / Story, Review
- Purpose, Outcomes, Anticipate
- 7x Practice, Credibility
- Intro, Q&A, Checklist
- Next Time, Feedback
- 1 Take-Away, Strong Close, Strong Opening, Middle to Close
- Text, Color, Images & Positioning
- Preparation, Script, Limited Scope
- Timing, Movements & Gestures, Energy
- Nerves, Make Friends, The Role of Slides, 3 Components
- Collection, Discussion

Blue Elephant Consulting
www.BlueElephantConsulting.com / 813.418.6970

Blue Elephant Consulting has created the **Clear Blue™ Presentation System** for creating and delivering powerful and memorable presentations. The contents of this book are based on lessons learned during the development of the Clear Blue system. Contact Blue Elephant Consulting to learn more about the Clear Blue presentation system.

Chapter 1

How To Give A Speech When You Are Not The One Doing The Talking

Chapter 1: How To Give A Speech When You Are Not The One Doing The Talking

They say that the world is getting smaller. I tend to believe that they are correct. However, there are still a lot of differences between here and there. When it comes to giving speeches, what this means is that there is a very good chance that at some point in the future you are going to find yourself being asked to give a speech to an audience who does not speak your language. **What's a speaker to do?**

The Power Of A Translator

I'd like to be able to tell you that one of those "learn a new language" programs that we see advertised all the time on the Internet would be your ticket to being able to deliver your speech in whatever tongue your audience speaks. However, that would not be the case. You're going to have to **call in some assistance** and that will take the form of an interpreter.

The way that this is going to work is that you will be on stage delivering your speech and the interpreter will then take what you said and speak it to the audience in a language that they understand. This will boost the importance of public speaking that you are doing. As you can well imagine, **this will have a dramatic impact on exactly how you end up giving your speech**.

What you are going to want to try to do is to get in touch with the person who will be your interpreter **before it is time for you to deliver your speech**. There are a number of different things that you'll want to talk with them about. If your speech uses any technical phrases or terms, these will be critical to share with them because they may not translate easily.

3 Tips For Making A Translated Speech Better

So it turns out that working with your interpreter is the key to successfully giving a speech to an audience that does not speak your language. Well ok then. Just exactly **what should you talk with the interpreter about** when you have the chance? I would suggest three different things:

- **Create A Script:** If you are like me, you may "wing" most of your presentations. It turns out that this is not a good idea when your speech is going to have to be interpreted. Instead, what you are going to want to do is to create a "script" for your presentation. You are going to want to use to provide your interpreter with a sense of the flow of your speech. Your script will allow them to become comfortable with what you are going to be saying before it has to be interpreted.
- **Allow Proper Time:** Guess what – an interpreted speech takes longer to give. No matter if your interpreter is performing a simultaneous translation or if they are translating what you just said, a translation is going to slow down your speech. When you are planning your speech you need to realize this and allow extra time. You will probably also have to shorten your speech in order to fit it into your allocated time.
- **Pick Your Word Carefully:** One of the most important things that you are going to have to realize about giving a speech that is going to be translated is that the actual words that you use will be more important than ever. What this means is that you'll want to stay away from using any words that may have a double meaning in your language – they will pose a challenge to the translator to get right. You need to be sure that you are

17

going to be able to clearly say all of the words in your speech – if you mumble or slur words, then your interpreter won't be able to do his or her job.

What All Of This Means For You

Let's face it – gearing up to give a speech takes a lot of effort. In today's interconnected world we will eventually be called on to deliver a speech to an audience that doesn't speak our language and **what was a lot of effort just got a whole lot harder**.

The good news is that you don't have to learn your audience's language in order to be able to communicate with them. Instead, **you can use an interpreter** — this one of the benefits of public speaking. Meeting with your interpreter before you give your speech is critical. You are going to have to create a script for your speech so that your interpreter can get comfortable with it long before you give it. When you are delivering your speech and being interpreted be sure to make sure that you've allocated enough time and that you and your interpreter are comfortable with all of the words that you are using.

The great thing about interpreters is that **they can open up the entire world to hear what we have to say**. However, we need to understand that giving a speech with the help of an interpreter means that we will have additional work to do. Take the time to carefully plan your interpreted speech and you'll be able to successfully reach a much larger audience with your message.

Chapter 2

How Public Speakers Can Minimize Their Accent

Chapter 2: How Public Speakers Can Minimize Their Accent

I just happen to speak English. I'd like to be able to tell you that I speak it very well; however, that's really up to other people to decide. What I can tell you is that it is the only language that I speak fluently and it's the language that I've always spoken. This provides me with **an unfair advantage** over many other speakers – they have accents that can distract an audience when they are speaking in English. What can they do in order to become more effective speakers?

It Turns Out That Your Accent Is Not A Problem

So what is it going to take in order to allow someone who grew up speaking a language that was not English to maximize the importance of public speaking and**effectively communicate** with an audience in English? It turns out, somewhat surprisingly, your accent is not going to be a problem.

There are a lot of great examples of successful famous people who speak with a heavy accent. Antonio Banderas is the one that pops into my mind first. Yes, these people have an accent, but it really makes them memorable – **it's not a distraction**. How have they managed to accomplish this? It turns out that they've discovered the secret to speaking good English: mastering the sounds of English.

It turns out that the English that everyone wants to hear has a pattern to it. This pattern is made up of **specific "pitch" and "rhythms"**. Speakers who's native language is not English can still speak in a way that will **connect with their audience** if they can learn to deliver their words in a manner that will be harmonious to the ear of their English-speaking audience.

It's All About How You Say It

One of reasons that non-native speakers of English have such a problem with the language is because their ears **have not been trained** to hear the basic sound patterns that make up the English language. What is going to have to be learned is how to place stress within a sentence and then how to manage both the beats and the rhythms of the English language.

A lot of the difficulties that non-native speaker of English run into **starts in the classroom**. There they are taught each word of English individually. However, in the real world when we are speaking English, we don't pronounce each word separately. Rather, we tend to run them together. One way to describe how English is spoken is to describe what we do as using melodic sound units.

What this all means for a non-native English speaker is that in order to speak English well, **they need to retrain their ears**. They need to find ways to listen to the melody of the sound units and then hear the words within. Native English speakers tend to shorten and contract words so that they can slide them together in order to create melodies.

What All Of This Means For You

If you didn't grow up speaking English, then learning to speak English later on in life can be quite a challenge. However, even if you do learn all of the words that make up the English language, you still have a big challenge ahead of you: **minimizing your accent**. What you need to realize is that you don't have to eliminate your accent, you just need to learn how to match how other people speak English in order to gain the benefits of public speaking.

It turns out that the secret to speaking English even if you do have an accent, is to **discover the melody of English**. When native speakers speak English, they use a specific pitch and rhythm. Words are shortened and contracted in order to slide them together. Mastering this technique will allow speakers with accents to be understood by their audience.

When we give a speech, we work hard to deliver the best speech possible. We don't want something like an accent to stand in our way. We want to be able to connect with our audience. Learning how English "sounds" to an audience and then taking steps to match this sound is the key to **minimizing the impact of our accent**. Follow these suggestions and you'll permit your next audience to focus on your speech, not your accent.

Chapter 3

Bouncing Back From A
Really Bad Speech

Chapter 3: Bouncing Back From A Really Bad Speech

I'd like to think that if we all realized the importance of public speaking and took enough time to prepare for every speech that we give then **each speech would be a success**. However, that's not the way that life works. There will be times that we give speeches where things just don't work out. We'll end up giving a bad speech. When that happens we generally feel quite bad about it. What should we do now?

What To Right After Giving A Bad Speech

Have you ever had a car come up from behind you really fast and all of sudden it is the only thing that you can see in your rear view mirror? Well, when you give a bad speech it seems to get larger and larger in your memory and pretty soon **it's the only thing that you can think of**. What you need to do right off the bat is to put it into perspective. Blowing a speech just means that you gave a bad speech, it does not mean that you are bad speaker or that you will never give a good speech again.

Instead of wallowing in self-pity, what you need to do is to sit yourself down and **give what happened some serious thought**. Your goal should be to analyze what went right with your speech (something always goes right) and then what went wrong. Your goal needs to be to learn from this bad experience. There are a lot of different ways to go about conducting this evaluation. Sometimes there are completed session evaluation forms, or you can ask a member of the audience what they thought, there may even be a video of your speech. Make sure that you are specific in your analysis – exactly what did you do that you never want to repeat again?

Once you understand what went wrong with your speech, your next step has to be to understand **why it happened**. In all honesty, more often than not what you are going to discover is that most of our bad speeches are a result of simply not taking the time to prepare correctly, There could also be personal factors such as not getting enough sleep or being distracted by the size of the crowd that could also be throwing you off.

How To Bounce Back From Giving A Bad Speech

One bad speech should not cause you to give up speaking forever. Instead, what you need to do is to get back up on that horse. The first thing that you are going to need to do is to **create a plan**. What you are going to want to do is to create a plan that will prevent the things that caused your last speech to bomb to never happen again. You need to be very specific with your plan – make sure that you spell out exactly what you will be doing and when you will do it.

Of course one thing that you are going to have to do after giving a bad speech will be to **get back up on the stage**. You are going to want to do this as quickly as possible. The good news is that you don't have to repeat the speech that gave you so much trouble or even speak in a similar situation. What you are going to be trying to do is to rebuild your confidence as a speaker. No matter if it's small steps, just the fact that you are taking any steps is good news.

Every time you give a speech, you need to understand you are repairing some of the damage that the bad speech did. You are going to want to **measure your progress**. Take the time to record your speeches and ask members of your audience for feedback. As you see evidence that you are getting better, your self confidence will start to improve. If you have any speaking strategies that don't seem to be working for you, take the time to modify them.

What All Of This Means For You

Life is unfair. What this means for us speakers is that there will be times that **we give speeches that fall flat on their face**. This can be rough on us when it happens. However, the good news is that it is not the end of the world.

When we give a bad speech, we need to remember the benefits of public speaking and **pick ourselves up again**. We can accomplish this by putting our bad performance in perspective. We need to take the time to figure out what went wrong – and what we did correctly. This all leads to us troubleshooting the speech that failed – what happened and why? After you know what went wrong, you need to start to prepare for the future. This includes creating a plan, getting back before an audience, and then measuring how much better you did.

As with all such things in life, there will be some point in the future that **you will give a speech that does not go so well**. When this happens, you need to get back up, dust yourself off, and then get back in the speaking ring. Having the skills to turn a bad speech into a valuable learning experience is what it takes to use this kind of experience to become an even better speaker.

Chapter 4

Learn To Read Your Next Audience
Like A Book

Chapter 4: Learn To Read Your Next Audience Like A Book

The quality of your next speech will not be determined by the amount of effort that you put into your PowerPoint / Keynote slides. It won't be determined by your clever use of pauses and hand gestures. Instead, your level of success will depend on **how well you are able to connect with your audience**. It turns out that it's not their job to connect with you (although that is what you want to have happen). Instead, due to the importance of public speaking it's your job to connect with them. Do you know how to do this?

3 Tips For Learning How To Read Your Next Audience

As we give our next speech, we want to be able to understand what our audience is thinking. The better that we understand what is going on in their heads, the more easily we can **adjust our speech to meet their needs**. In order to connect with our audience and deliver the speech that they deserve, there are three things that we need to learn how to do.

In order to get our audience to wake up and participate in your speech, you need to **ask them a question**. This will show you that they are following what you are saying. If you ask a question and you don't get an answer from your audience, then you know that you've got trouble on your hands. What you need to do then is to rephrase the question and ask it again.

Next you need to <u>study where your audience's eyes are going</u>. If they are not looking at you then they are trying to tell you something. Blank expressions or audience members who are staring off into space are always a bad sign. If you see this happening, then it's a clear sign that as a speaker you need to **change the approach that you are currently using**. If on the other hand you discover that your audience is making eye contact with you, then you can take that as a form of acceptance for what you are telling them.

Finally, you are going to want to do a good job of making eye contact with your audience. This means that you need to **pick a few people out of your audience and make eye contact with them one by one**. If you don't get any reaction from them as you make eye contact with them, then it means that you are not moving them with your words. Your audience's faces reveal what they are thinking. You want them to have expressions that indicate they they are participating in your speech.

What All Of This Means For You

Speakers need to be able to determine what their audience is thinking while they are giving their speech. The reason that this is so important is because if it turns out that we're losing our audience to boredom or some other distraction, then one of the benefits of public speaking is that we can **adjust how we are giving our speech**.

Learning **how to read an audience** is a critical speaking skill. We can always halt our speech and ask our audience a question. This is a great way to both wake them up and get them involved in the speech. We need to be aware of what our audience is doing with their eyes – are they looking at us? If they aren't, then we have a problem on our hands. Finally, we need to make eye contact with members of our audience.

Giving a speech is not a one-way path. Every time you deliver a speech, your audience will be **telling you what they think of the speech** as you deliver it. You need to understand the language that they will be speaking and then you need to take action based on it. Read your audience and deliver the speech that they want to hear.

Chapter 5

How To Deal With Speaking Anxiety When It Comes

Chapter 5: How To Deal With Speaking Anxiety When It Comes

Speaking is hard work. As though it wasn't hard enough, despite us knowing about the importance of public speaking, there is that pesky issue of **speaking anxiety**. What's that you say? It's when we start to understand that we're going to be standing in front of a (potentially large) group of people and will be expected to both remember what we want to say and do a good job of delivering our message. When our bodies start to realize what we are planning on doing, that's when the real fun starts…!

What Is Speaking Anxiety?

So what is this thing that we call speaking anxiety anyway? Think back to the last time that you gave a speech. Do you remember if you had any flushing going on (becoming red in the neck, face, or upper chest area]? Did you experience any shaking of your body? If so, then **you've been experiencing the physical symptoms of speaking anxiety**.

This anxiety can take on a number of different forms. It can **play havoc with the way that we speak**. We can end up repeating words, unintentionally using filler words, and stuttering. It can also affect how we deliver a speech by making us fidgety, causing us to break eye contact, along with swaying and pacing. What we are all experiencing is a set of the body's "fight or flight" response mechanisms.

Our body has realized what we are planning on doing – standing in front of a group of people and delivering a speech. It's letting us know that **it would rather be doing something else**, in fact it would prefer to be doing almost anything else! The good news is that everything that you are experiencing is a perfectly natural response to a stressful situation. Now all you have to do is to find out what you need to do in order to counter it...

How Can We Deal With Speaking Anxiety?

In order to deal with the physical symptoms of speaking anxiety, **you need to take physical steps to counter them**. One of the simplest is to make sure that you are breathing correctly. You want to make sure that you are breathing both slowly and deeply. Additionally, you are going to want to make sure that you are breathing properly by filling your lower abdomen by inhaling slowly through your nose and exhaling slowly through your mouth – so called "belly breathing".

Another effect of speaking anxiety is that **your body's core temperature gets raised**. You are going to want to take steps to lower it. One way to go about doing this while you are heading for the stage is to place something cool in your hands. Something that will accomplish this is a cold bottle of water.

Pacing and swaying are all symptoms of a speaker having too much energy and not knowing what to do with it. In order to get rid of these distracting movements, **we need to find a way to channel that energy in other directions**. One way to do this is to gesture broadly during your speech and then step towards your audience. Another way is to secretly squeeze your toes – it will burn off energy and nobody will ever be the wiser!

What All Of This Means For You

One of the facts of life is that despite the benefits of public speaking, **speaking will make all of us anxious**. Some more than others. We would like to be able to focus on our speech and not how our bodies are rebelling against the speech that we are planning on giving. This means that we're going to have to take steps to calm ourselves down.

In order to overcome our natural **"fight or flight"** instincts that take over when our bodies realize that we are planning on giving a speech, we need to take a number of steps. These are all designed to put control of our body back into our hands.

The first thing that we need to do is to **get our breathing under control**. This includes both remembering to breath and making sure that we breathe correctly. Next we need to lower our core body temperature by getting in contact with something that is cooler than we are. Finally, we have to find a way to burn off the excess energy that we are dealing with.

There is nothing that we can do about becoming nervous about our next speaking opportunity. This is just a fact of life. Our bodies will react in exactly the way that we expect them to – they are going to display all of the hallmarks of **being nervous and under pressure**. It is our job to realize this and take steps to calm ourselves down and get our bodies back under control. Do this right and nobody will ever know just how nervous you really are.

Your audience just wants to hear your speech – **they don't really want to see that you are nervous**. It's your responsibility to deliver the best speech possible and this means that you need to find ways to make sure that nobody is going to know just how much pressure you are under. Follow the suggestions that we've outlined and the next time that you give a speech you will be the only one who knows just how nervous you really are.

Chapter 6

Eye See What You Are Talking About

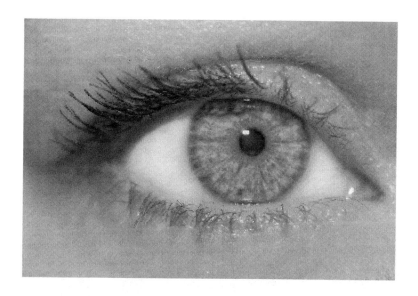

Chapter 6: Eye See What You Are Talking About

I've got a quick question for you: what's the most important thing that speaker can do during a presentation? Give up? The answer is to **form a bond with your audience**. This will only happen if your audience believes that they really "get you" – that you understand them and that your message has been hand crafted just for them. This is what the importance of public speaking is all about. If you want to make this happen next time you speak, then you are going to have to learn to use eye contact correctly...

Eye Contact Is All About Understanding

What a lot of speakers don't seem to understand when they are delivering a speech is that each speech that we give is really **a two-way street**. They get caught up in all of the techniques that we all try to use in order to have a great presentation. What they forget is that if you don't know what your audience is thinking, then you'll never be able to give a speech that meets their needs.

What we need to do when we give a speech is to **look into our audience's eyes while we are talking**. The reason that we want to be doing this is because our eyes are one of the most communicative parts of the human face. When you are looking into your audience's eyes you'll be able to detect if they are smiling, frowning, or if they are bored, excited, or even if they are understanding what you are saying. This is critical information for you to have so that you can take action.

The reason that I'm saying that your next speech has to be a two-way street is because when you look into your audience's eyes, they'll be telling you what they currently think about the speech that you are giving. If the reaction is not the one that you wanted to get, then **you are going to have to adjust what you are saying** and how you are saying it.

Good Eye Contact Helps You To Relax

As speakers we can become very tense and nervous when it comes time for us to give a speech. One of the reasons that this happens is that we are focused on ourselves. If we start to understand that we need to take the time to study the eyes of our audience, then all of a sudden we'll have less time to think about ourselves. The natural result of this will be that **we will become much more calmer**.

If we are able to build good eye contact with our audience, then we will have effectively started to **build rapport with them**. Your audience will be expecting you to look into their eyes. This is one of the ways that they go about judging the truthfulness of what you are saying.

Now comes the question of just exactly how you can go about making good eye contact with your audience. The best way to do this is to look directly at one member of your audience and **deliver a full thought** while looking at them. A great side effect of this is that everyone around this person is going to think that you are really looking at them. Once you are done with this thought, shift your gaze to another audience member and repeat the process. Read their eyes as you speak and determine if they are understanding what you are telling them.

What All Of This Means For You

The next time that you give a speech, your goal has to be to find a way to use your speech **to maximize the benefits of public speaking and really connect with your audience**. One of the best ways to go about doing this is to learn to make effective eye contact with your audience.

One of the most important things that you are going to have to learn to do as an effective speaker will be to **read your audience**. Are they understanding what you are sharing with them? Making good eye contact with your audience is a great way to go about doing this. Additionally, by spending your time focusing on making good eye contact with your audience, you can distract yourself and this will allow you to be less nervous when you are giving your speech.

A speech is a very special type of conversation. You are trying to communicate your thoughts and ideas to a room full of people. However, even though there may be many of them, you want each member of your audience to believe that **you are talking only to them**. Learning how to effectively use eye contact is a great way to go about making this happen.

Each and every one of us wants to become a better speaker. In order to make this happen we are always looking for the techniques that we can implement to reach that next level of speaking. The good news in this case is that it is actually quite easy to get there – all we have to do is to practice and **improve our eye contact**. Once we master this skill, we'll be able to connect with our audiences and they'll be able to let us know how we're doing.

Chapter 7

What Happens To Your Speech When You're Done Talking?

Chapter 7: What Happens To Your Speech When You're Done Talking?

Creating a speech is hard work. You take the time to understand who you will be talking to, what they want you to talk about, and how long you'll have to talk. You then craft a fantastic opening line, outline a speech that will allow you to make whatever point you want to make, and then you start to practice it. <u>You practice, practice, practice</u>. Finally, the big day comes and you give your speech. Hopefully it went well because we all know about the importance of public speaking. **Now just what the heck are you going to do with this speech that you've spent so much time creating?**

File It

You do realize that you know more about this speech right now than you will ever know about it in the future, right? What this means is that if you don't take steps to record how you delivered this speech, then **this information is going to be lost forever.**

If you are like me, then you probably didn't write your speech out. Instead, you may have written out the important parts (the opening and the closing), and then you pretty much worked off of an outline for the rest of what you wanted to say. That outline that served you so well now is going to be your downfall going forward – **you won't be able to remember how you filled in the gaps later on.**

Now is the time for you to sit down and, gasp!, **write out your speech**. The reason that you're doing this is not so that you can read it to someone in the future, but rather so that you can remember what you said. By writing out each word in your speech you can now file it away and if you ever want to give it again in the future you can just get it out, read what you've written, and then you'll be able to remember exactly what you wanted to say.

Deliver It Again

Once again, you are currently the best person in the world to give this speech. What this means is that now is the time for you to **deliver it as many times as you possibly can**. Just think about it – you really won't have to practice!

In order to do this correctly, you are going to have to take a long hard look at **what the topic of your speech was**. The next audience that you'll be giving it to will be different from your first audience. What this means is that you are going to have to be willing to make changes to your speech. Your goal needs to be to find an audience that is as similar to your original audience as possible in order to minimize the number of changes that you have to make.

Once again depending on the content of your speech, you may be able to change it so that it can **work with a completely different audience**. For example you might want to try to see if it would be an appropriate speech to give to at a storytelling event. Even business speeches can be transformed and turned into interesting stores with a moral that can keep a storytelling audience transfixed.

Make Yourself An Expert

You spent the time learning everything that you needed to know. What this means is that for a brief, glorious moment in time, you are probably the one person on this plant **who knows the most about what you are talking about**. Since you've gone to all of the effort to achieve this lofty goal, perhaps you should make the most of it?

A lot of us speakers get tapped on the shoulder every once in a while when someone that knows us needs someone to step in and give a speech. Since we generally know these people, more often than not **we end up saying yes to them**. It's only after we say yes that we realize just how much effort creating a speech for their event is going to take – or how little time there is to get ready!

Now that you've mastered the speech that you just gave, perhaps it's time for it to become your **"back pocket speech"**. This is the speech that you know so well that you can just whip it out and deliver it any time that someone needs you to give a speech? Do a bit of documentation and find some opportunities to practice it some more and you'll be good to go.

Go Online

Welcome to the 21st Century! The day and age that we find ourselves living in presents us with new opportunities that were not available to us even just a few years ago. Once of these opportunities is, of course, **the Internet**. If you use this resource correctly, your speech can live forever.

What this means is that you're going to have to do a bit of preplanning. You'll need to make arrangements to **have your speech taped** when you give it. After that is done, some post processing will probably be required in order to get it ready for the world to see.

Having gotten all of this taken care of, you can now look for places to share it one the web. The obvious choice will be YouTube. However, once you've gotten that taken care of, you might want to do some more looking around. Based on the topic of your speech I'm sure that there are **many other sites** that would be interested in having new video to show their visitors.

What All Of This Means For You

Nobody ever told you that creating a speech was going to be something that was easy to do. However, this is something that we all know how to go about doing and so we do it. Once we've done all of the required work and we've delivered our speech, **what can we do with the speech now to maximize the benefits of public speaking?**

It turns out that the answer to that question is quite a lot. The first thing that we need to do is to take steps to **record just exactly what we said for future reference**. Next, we can deliver it in other settings and we can take the time to become an expert and create our very own back pocket speech. Finally, we can harness the power of the Internet and post a video of us giving our speech.

If you were to think of your next speech as being a sort of a living thing, then you can consider the actual delivery of the speech as being the birthing process. Once a speech is born, now you have to **find different ways to raise it**. The possibilities that we've discussed here are just the tip of the iceberg. You created the speech, now set it free!

Chapter 8

What You've Never Been Taught About Being A Successful Speaker

Chapter 8: What You've Never Been Taught About Being A Successful Speaker

Once you get over the shakes and nerves that go along with standing in front of a group of people and delivering a speech, your next big challenge is going to be **finding ways to get better** in order to maximize importance of public speaking. Deep down inside, what each one of us would like is if we could find ways to make the effort that we put into each speech make us just a little bit better. It turns out that there are three things that we can be doing that will make this happen.

You Are Going To Need A Mentor

If you are going to have any hope of becoming better, then you are going to need some help to get there. What this comes down to is simple – you are going to need to find yourself a mentor. If we were back in school, an mentor would be assigned to you. Sorry – that doesn't happen anymore. Now you are going to have to get up and go out and **find yourself a mentor**.

Finding someone who is willing to be your mentor is a big deal. However, you need to keep in mind that they won't be your mentor forever. Mentors will change over your lifetime as both your and their needs continue to change. Remember that it is your responsibly to make it easy for your mentor to work with you. Additionally, since they are willing to work with you, you need to always be looking for ways to make them more successful also.

It's All About Your Reputation

If you want to get better at this speaking thing, then you are going to have to deliver some speeches. This means that people are going to have to be able to locate you and then decide that they want you to come and talk to their audience. What's going to make this easier to accomplish is if you have a good reputation.

In the world of speaking your reputation is going to be built on many different things. There will be simple things such as showing up on time, only using the time that you've been allocated, etc. However, there will be more subtle things also such as your ability to connect with your audience. We need to keep in mind that if we don't have a positive reputation, then it's going to be very hard to get speaking opportunities. One wrong move and you can end up trashing your speaking reputation.

Do You Have Goals?

If you are going to want to become better then you need to take the time to sit down and create some goals. For you see, if you don't have a clear vision of where you want to get to, then you're never going to be able to get there. The reason that we create goals is so that when we are in the middle of something and we're wondering why we're making the effort to do a task, we can remember what our goal is and it will give us the strength to carry on.

All too often I run into speakers who tell me that they do have goals. However, when I ask them what their goals are, they start to stammer and look up into the sky as they try to remember just exactly what their goals are. Look, if you are going to create speaking goals for yourself, do it the right way. You've heard it before but it never hurts to hear it again: a goal must be measurable, identifiable, attainable, specific, and, here's the most important part, in writing. If this is what your goals look like, then you should be all set to achieve them.

What All Of This Means For You

Becoming better at what we do is something that all of us want. When it comes to delivering speeches, things are no different. We'd all like to become better public speakers so that we can share the benefits of public speaking, the challenge that we all face is that it's not always clear what areas of our speaking we need to be working on.

In order to improve the quality of the speeches that we give, we need to first go out and find a mentor. This will be a person who can give us advice on how the speeches that we are giving are going over. We need to keep in mind that time changes everything and so we may need to change mentors over time. Next we need to realize that it's going to be our reputation as a public speaker that is going to get us our next speaking gig. Finally, in order to become a better speaker we need to have real goals that we can work towards achieving.

We all want to become the best public speaker that we can be. What we need to realize is that it's a journey from where we are to where we want to be. This is a journey that we won't be able to make by ourselves, we're going to need mentors. However, if we follow these suggestions then eventually we're going to discover that we have become the speaker that we knew that we could be.

Chapter 9

3 Very Small Ways To Become A Better Speaker

Chapter 9: 3 Very Small Ways To Become A Better Speaker

I don't mind telling you that **I'd like to become a better speaker**. In fact, I'd be willing to bet that because of the importance of public speaking you pretty much feel the same way. However, we always face the big challenge – what do we need to do in order to become better? Should we run away for a week in the woods with a speaking guru? Perhaps, but it turns out that there are a number of small things that we can do that will have a big impact on how good of a speaker we become.

Don't Worry, Be Happy

All too often I run into speakers who are not happy. When I talk with them and try to find out what's up, more often than not what I discover is that **somebody has done something that this person feels has wronged them**. What they have forgotten is that ultimately, they are the ones who are in control of how they feel and if they are going to feel happy, then it's going to be all up to them.

Being a speaker is tough work – it truly takes a lot of energy out of all of us. If you choose to be unhappy, then you are going to discover that **being unhappy also takes a lot of work**. You'll have less energy to give to your speeches. It's not worth it so don't be unhappy. Develop a positive attitude and you'll be ready to all of the opportunities and challenges that come along with being a speaker.

Did You Remember To Smile Today?

I don't know about you, but I sure wish that I had the ability to control other people. It just seems like everything would go that much easier because everyone would be doing exactly what I wanted them to do. I don't have that ability, but **I do have the ability to change other people's moods**. All I have to do is to smile at them.

When you smile at someone they really have no choice about what they are going to do next. **They are almost forced to smile back at you**. When they do this, something happens and all of a sudden they just feel better. What this means is that they now associate you with feeling better. From that association great things can happen. And it all started with just a smile.

Don't Forget Your Sense Of Humor

There are a lot of serious things that we deal with in this life. However, if we don't have a sense of humor then when the unexpected happens **we are going to be poorly equipped to handle it**. If when something happens, you are just going to stand there and look upset, then that is exactly how your audience is going to be feeling.

Instead, what you need to do is to develop the ability to roll with events as they occur. Look at everything that happens to you and find the lighter side of it. I'm not talking about trying to memorize jokes here, rather I'm talking about having the ability to see events as they unfold and to **make your audience laugh about being part of it**. If you can get good at this, then you'll be able to keep your audience focused on you even as the unexpected happens.

What All Of This Means For You

When we think about becoming a better speaker, I'm pretty sure that we all picture going off to some military style boot camp where drill sergeants run us through speaking exercises day and night until we can do them in our sleep. Such a place may exist, but it turns out that **becoming a better speaker and maximizing the benefits of public speaking is actually much easier to accomplish**.

The first thing that we need to understand is that **we control our mood – nobody else does**. What this means for you is that if you want to be happy, it's going to be up to you to make it happen, not someone else. Next, we have the ability to influence how other people feel. All we have to do is to smile at them and they'll smile back at us. This makes everyone feel better. Finally, when you head off to speak, make sure that you take your sense of humor along. We don't control the world so as things happen, make sure that you and your audience can laugh at them.

When you realize that becoming a better speaker is not only fairly easy to do, but is also in your hands to accomplish, all of sudden this starts to seem like **it might be something that you could accomplish**. The three things that we've discussed are easy to do. Give it a try and see what comes of it!

Chapter 10

How To Make Your Next Speech Unforgettable

Chapter 10: How To Make Your Next Speech Unforgettable

In order for the effort that we put into creating and delivering a speech to all be worth it, we need to get something out of the presentation. Yes, if you are being paid to speak, then you are getting something, but even then we speakers want more. What we want is **for our audience to be moved to action by what we have told them**. How to make this happen during your next speech is what we all want to know how to do.

The Challenge Of Trying To Be Remembered

If our audience can't remember what we've told them despite the importance of public speaking, then whose fault is it –theirs or ours? Yes, it may be ours but your audience is not going to be helping you out very much. When we use too many slides as a part of our presentation, **we tend to overwhelm our audience**. A number of studies have been done on audiences in order to determine just exactly how much of what we told them they remember after we're done. The results are pretty dismal. Just a mere 48 hours after a speech, <u>audiences were able to recall only about 20% of the slides that were presented</u>.

So what's going on here? Are we really that boring? The answer, thankfully, is no. One of the biggest problems that our audiences are facing is the simple fact that we've selected a common look & feel for the material that we are presenting to them. What this tends to do is to end up **making everything that we present to them look the same**. When the presentation is over and done with, they'll be hard pressed to be able to distinguish between anything that was presented to them.

Finally, sitting in a darkened room listening to a person talk at you from the stage makes it hard for anyone to remember what was said. **This is just not a conducive environment for memory retention**. If we are not careful, then what's going to happen is that members of our audience are going to become distracted by other things and we'll lose them and they won't be able to remember what we've told them.

How To Help Your Audience Recall Your Message

The good news about this audience memory retention problem that we are facing is that there are solutions for it. First off, **we have the responsibility to keep shaking up our audience**. The one thing that we don't want to do is to present them with too much of the same look and feel for our material. We need to give them the unusual – our material has to be different from what they were expecting. This means varying the graphics, the colors, the font sizes, etc.

Next, we need to take steps to **involve our audience in our presentation**. If we just present slide after slide of material that we developed ourselves, then our audience is going to go to sleep because they are not involved. However, if we take a different approach and leave some material out and force our audience to be the ones who fill in the blanks, then all of a sudden they've made a contribution. Studies have shown that when you involve your audience in this way, their retention of what you told them goes way up.

Finally, we need to understand that how we remember things is not all about what we heard or saw. Instead, a big part of it has to do with **what we felt during the presentation**. This means that you are going to have to take into account how your material is going to make your audience feel. The more of an emotional response that you can get out of them, the higher the likelihood is that they will remember what you told them.

What All Of This Means For You

It's not easy pulling together a speech, practicing it, and then delivering it in front of a live audience. However, as long as we are going to go to all of this effort, we want to be able to achieve a measurable result – we want our audience to be moved to action to do something. However, **all too often this does not happen**. What's a speaker to do?

There are a number of different reasons why our speech might not make our audience understand the benefits of public speaking and then want to stand up and go out and change the world. Chief among these are our audience's inability to remember what we said even just 48 hours after our speech is over. What we need to do is to take steps in order to make our speeches more memorable. The first thing that we can do is to introduce the unusual into our material – **the unusual gets remembered**. Additionally, getting your audience to participate by filling in missing information can boost their retention. Finally, how your audience feels during your speech can have a big impact on how much of it they remember. Craft your speech to generate the biggest emotional response possible.

As speakers we are in the unique position that **our speeches can change the world**. However, they are not going to do that if our audience can't remember what we've told them. For your next presentation shake things up a bit and make sure that what you are presenting is so bold and so unique that even days after your speech is over your audience will still remember it and be talking about it.

Chapter 11

How To Become A Speaker Who Is An Online Leader

Chapter 11: How To Become A Speaker Who Is An Online Leader

Remember the old days? Those were the days when we'd write a speech, travel to where we were going to be giving it, wait for our time to talk, get up on stage and deliver our speech, and then drive home? Well, welcome to the 21st Century. Now that so much can be done online, we no longer have to drive anywhere – your next speech could be delivered online. The importance of public speaking has never been greater. However, this is a brave new world – **do you know how to be a leader in this space?**

Be Interesting

A key point about any speech that you are going to be giving is that nobody is going to take the time to come listen to you **if you are not interesting**. Every speech that you give, even if it is online, has to be telling your audience how they can go out and do great things. You have to be willing to take risks when you deliver you speeches and by doing this you can change the status quo.

Deliver More Than You Promised

When I show up to hear someone speak, I generally have a set of expectations. If the speaker meets those expectations, then I leave the speech feeling as though I got my money's worth (even if I didn't pay anything to attend). However, on those rare times that a speaker over delivers and I end up getting a lot more from the speech than I had expected, these are the times that I leave feeling pumped up and excited. When you deliver an online speech, you'll want to over deliver. This can be as simple as sending a copy of your slides to everyone who attended the presentation after it's over. Give them more than they expected and they'll always come back for more.

Don't Forget The Real World

It can be all too easy to slide into the virtual world of online presentations. We can't see our audience and we generally don't have to dress up from the waist down. However, we all need to keep in mind that **we are presenting to real people** no matter where in this big world they are located. This means that when we are not presenting, our time would be well spent going out into the real world and meeting the people who attend our online presentations. Put a name with a login and find out what they really think about you. This is the best way to become a better online presenter.

Say Good Things About Other People

As a presenter, you want people to be saying good things about you and your online presentations. In order to make this happen you, of course, need to do a good job. However, something else that you need to do is to **take the time to complement other people**. For you see, when you complement other people, your audience will see you as being a bigger person and the person that you complement will get the word that you are saying good things about them and may return the favor. Make sure that when you complement someone you are very specific: tell people why they should pay attention to this person. This shows that you've been paying attention to them.

Make Sure That You Have A Vision

Finally, when you are making an online presentation, it all has to mean something. You are giving this presentation for a reason. Yes, you might be getting paid to do it, but you choose to take the time and be online right now and talk about this topic as opposed to all of the other things that you could be doing with your time. Why? Hopefully it is because you really believe in what you are talking about. When **you believe in what you are talking about** it comes through in your speech and your audience will start to believe in it also.

What All Of This Means For You

The world is changing. Whereas we used to travel to a location to deliver a speech, that is no longer necessary. Now, thanks to the amazing technology that we have available to us, we can simply go online and deliver a speech and share the benefits of public speaking with an audience. However, this changes everything for us. **How can we lead an audience when we can't even see them?**

The answer is that **we need to make sure that we are interesting and that we're talking about interesting things**. When we make a presentation we need to over deliver and provide our audience with more information than they were expecting. We have to keep in mind that even though we can't see them, our audience is made up of real people and we need to go out and meet them. We can generate good karma for ourselves if we pay complements to other people. Finally, we need to have a vision and we need to allow it to come through in our speech.

Yes, moving into a new age where we can now make our presentations online is both daunting and just a bit scary. However, we can't stop progress and so **we all need to learn how to not only survive, but thrive in this new world**. As long as we are going to be making presentations online, we need to learn how to be leaders in this new online world. Follow the suggestions that we've covered and you'll soon be the master of this new world.

Chapter 12

How To Grow Your Speaking Abilities

Chapter 12: How To Grow Your Speaking Abilities

As speakers we all start out the same: we get asked to give our first speech, we may be nervous but somehow we summon up the strength to get up there in front of everyone and actually give a speech! Now that that is over, **we'd like to get better at this speech giving thing** because we understand the importance of public speaking. What's a speaker to do when we want to become a better speaker?

Acceptance Speeches

One of the things that it can be hard for speakers who are staring out to wrap their heads around is that the opportunity to practice giving speech **can come in many different forms**. Yes, we are all aware of the "stand in front of an audience and give a speech" type of speech; however, it turns out that there are a number of different forms that speeches can take and we need to be willing to keep our eyes open.

One such opportunity is **the acceptance speech**. We are always being rewarded for something that we've done. These may or may not be big formal affairs. However, each one of these opportunities provides you with yet another chance to practice your public speaking skills. You'll first need to thank the people who are giving you the award, then you'll need to thank the people who made this possible, and finally you'll need to wrap thing up by telling everyone why this recognition is meaningful to you.

Toasts / Roasts

I'm sure that we've all been at dining events where all of a sudden somebody starts **tapping on their water glass to get our attention**. Once they've done this, they stand up and proceed to offer a toast to some important person who is at the event. You may not have seen this as what it is, a speaking opportunity, but you should.

Toasts and roasts are very similar in nature. **They both call attention to a person who is present in the audience.** They very much encourage the audience to join in the speech with you. A toast is a celebration of something that the person has done or accomplished while a roast is designed to be humorous at the expense of the person being discussed. Both types of speeches require you to do some research in advance on the person that you'll be talking about.

TED Talks

With a little luck we all know what TED talks are. These are speeches that are limited to no more than 18 minutes; they are given without a lectern, and generally use few if any slides. The heart of a TED talk is **your ability to tell a good story**. The idea behind a TED talk is for you to give a speech that contains "ideas worth spreading".

No, you probably are not going to get invited out to California to give a TED talk in front of all of the important and / or famous people who show up for these things; however, **this does not mean that you can't give a TED talk**. First off, there is an offshoot of TED talks called TEDx which are locally produced and run versions of TED talks. They are not the original, but they are often quite good. If there is going to be one of these in your town, then you might want to sign up. Even if there is not, then the next time that you give a speech you might want to try to follow the rules for a TED talk just to find out if you could do it.

What All Of This Means For You

The good news about becoming a better speaker is that it is possible to do. What you are going to want to do is to **give more speeches** so that you can share the benefits of public speaking. However, it's not just good enough to give more speeches, what you are also going to have to do is to mix up the variety of speeches that you give. It turns out that this is also possible to do.

The trick to getting a chance to practice your public speaking is to realize that **speaking opportunities can take on a lot of different forms**. One such form is the acceptance speech. We are always getting recognized for something and if we use this opportunity correctly, we can practice giving a speech. Next comes toasts and roasts. These speaking opportunities can be dynamic and may be thrust upon us. We need to make sure that we've done our homework so that we'll be prepared. TED talks are also quite popular. We need to look for TEDx talks in our area or simply use TED techniques in our next speech.

Becoming a better speaker is something that takes time. We have to be willing to work at it. We never know when a speaking opportunity will show up and so **we need to be ready to seize it when it does**. Search out the different speaking opportunities that are available to you and then make the most of them!

It's from the forge of failure that the steel of success is formed.

Hard Work Does Not Guarantee Success, But Success Does Not Happen Without Hard Work.

- Dr. Jim Anderson

Create Speeches That Motivate Your Audiences And Get Your Message Heard!

Dr. Jim Anderson is available to provide training and coaching on the topics that are the most important to people who have to speak in public: how can I create a speech that people want to hear and how can I deliver in a way that will allow me to connect with my audience and get my point across to them?

Dr. Anderson believes that in order to both learn and remember what he says, speakers need to laugh. Each one of his speeches is full of fun and humor so that what he says "sticks" with everyone.

Dr. Anderson's Public Speaking Training Includes:

1. How to plan your next speech: pick your purpose and understand your audience.
2. What's the best way to get PowerPoint and Keynote to work with you, not against you?
3. What do you need to do when you are presenting in order to truly connect with your audience?

Dr. Jim Anderson presents over 100 speeches per year. To invite Dr. Anderson to speak at your event, contact him at:

Phone: 813-418-6970 or
Email: jim@BlueElephantConsulting.com

Speaking. Negotiating. Managing. Marketi

Photo Credits:

Cover - Robert Couse-Baker
https://www.flickr.com/photos/29233640@N07/

Chapter 1 – jeanbaptisteparis
https://www.flickr.com/photos/jeanbaptisteparis/

Chapter 2 - Satish Krishnamurthy
https://www.flickr.com/photos/unlistedsightings/

Chapter 3 - Lutz Koch
https://www.flickr.com/photos/elkaypics/

Chapter 4 - Pedro Ribeiro Simões
https://www.flickr.com/photos/pedrosimoes7/

Chapter 5 - Brandon Warren
https://www.flickr.com/photos/brandoncwarren/

Chapter 6 - Riccardo Cuppini
https://www.flickr.com/photos/cuppini/

Chapter 7 - Colette Saint Yves
https://www.flickr.com/photos/colettestyves/

Chapter 8 – alamosbasement
https://www.flickr.com/photos/alamosbasement/

Chapter 9 - Freddie Alequin
https://www.flickr.com/photos/falequin/

Chapter 10 - Brittany H.
https://www.flickr.com/photos/thelivelygirl/

Chapter 11 - Wies van Erp
https://www.flickr.com/photos/2a1_wies_van_erp/

Chapter 12 – motiqua
https://www.flickr.com/photos/motiqua/

Other Books By The Author

Product Management

- How Product Managers Can Sell More Of Their Product: Tips & Techniques For Product Managers To Better Understand How To Sell Their Product

- How Product Managers Can Sell More Of Their Product: Tips & Techniques For Product Managers To Better Understand How To Sell Their Product

- How To Create A Successful Product That Customers Will Want: Techniques For Product Managers To Boost Product Sales And Increase Customer Satisfaction

- What Product Managers Need To Know About World-Class Product Development: How Product Managers Can Create Successful Products

- How Product Managers Can Learn To Understand Their Customers: Techniques For Product Managers To Better Understand What Their Customers Really Want

- Product Management Secrets: Techniques For Product Managers To Boost Product Sales And Increase Customer Satisfaction

- Product Development Lessons For Product Managers: How Product Managers Can Create Successful Products

- Customer Lessons For Product Managers: Techniques For Product Managers To Better Understand What Their Customers Really Want

- Product Failure Lessons For Product Managers: Examples Of Products That Have Failed For Product Managers To Learn From

- Communication Skills For Product Managers: The Communication Skills That Product Managers Need To Know How To Use In Order To Have A Successful Product

- How To Have A Successful Product Manager Career: The Things That You Need To Be Doing TODAY In Order To Have A Successful Product Manager Career

- Product Manager Product Success: How to keep your product on track and make it become a success

- Killer Ways To Make Partnerships Work For Product Managers: Techniques For Product Managers To Find Ways To Work With Others In Order To Make Their Product Successful

Public Speaking

- Creating Speeches That Work: How To Create A Speech That Will Make Your Message Be Remembered Forever!

- How To Organize A Speech In Order To Make Your Point: How to put together a speech that will capture and hold your audience's attention

- Changing How You Speak To Overcome Your Fear Of Speaking: Change techniques that will transform a speech into a memorable event

- Delivering Excellence: How To Give Presentations That Make A Difference: Presentation techniques that will transform a speech into a memorable event

- Tools Speakers Need In Order To Give The Perfect Speech: What tools to use to create your next speech so that your message will be remembered forever!

- How To Create A Speech That Will Be Remembered

- Secrets To Organizing A Speech For Maximum Impact: How to put together a speech that will capture and hold your audience's attention

- How To Become A Better Speaker By Changing How You Speak: Change techniques that will transform a speech into a memorable event

- How To Give A Great Presentation: Presentation techniques that will transform a speech into a memorable event

- How To Rehearse In Order To Give The Perfect Speech: How to effectively rehearse your next speech to that your message be remembered forever!

- Secrets To Creating The Perfect Speech: How to create a speech that will make your message be remembered forever!

- Secrets To Organizing The Perfect Speech: How to organize the best speech of your life!

- Secrets To Planning The Perfect Speech: How to plan to give the best speech of your life

- How To Show What You Mean During A Presentation: How to use visual techniques to transform a speech into a memorable event

CIO Skills

- How CIOs Can Bring Business And IT Together: How CIOs Can Use Their Technical Skills To Help Their Company Solve Real-World Business Problems

- New IT Technology Issues Facing CIOs: How CIOs Can Stay On Top Of The Changes In The Technology That Powers The Company

- Keeping The Barbarians Out: How CIOs Can Secure Their Department and Company: Tips And Techniques For CIOs To Use In Order To Secure Both Their IT Department And Their Company

- What CIOs Need To Know In Order To Successfully Manage An IT Department: Decision Making Skills That Every CIO Needs To Have In Order To Be Able To Make The Right Choices

- Becoming A Powerful And Effective Leader: Tips And Techniques That IT Managers Can Use In Order To Develop Leadership Skills

- CIO Secrets For Growing Innovation: Tips And Techniques For CIOs To Use In Order To Make Innovation Happen In Their IT Department

- Your Success As A CIO Depends On How Well You Communicate: Tips And Techniques For CIOs To

Use In Order To Become Better Communicators

- What CIOs Need To Know About Working With Partners: Techniques For CIOs To Use In Order To Be Able To Successfully Work With Partners

- Critical CIO Management Skills: Decision Making Skills That Every CIO Needs To Have In Order To Be Able To Make The Right Choices

- How CIOs Can Make Innovation Happen: Tips And Techniques For CIOs To Use In Order To Make Innovation Happen In Their IT Department

- CIO Communication Skills Secrets: Tips And Techniques For CIOs To Use In Order To Become Better Communicators

- Managing Your CIO Career: Steps That CIOs Have To Take In Order To Have A Long And Successful Career

- CIO Business Skills: How CIOs can work effectively with the rest of the company!

IT Manager Skills

- Killer Staffing Skills Managers Need To Know: Tips And Techniques That Managers Can Use In Order

To Develop Leadership Skills

- How IT Managers Can Use New Technology To Meet Today's IT Challenges: Technologies That IT Managers Can Use In Order to Make Their Teams More Productive

- How To Build High Performance IT Teams: Tips And Techniques That IT Managers Can Use In Order To Develop Productive Teams

- Save Yourself, Save Your Job – How To Manage Your IT Career: Secrets That IT Managers Can Use In Order To Have A Successful Career

- Growing Your CIO Career: How CIOs Can Work With The Entire Company In Order To Be Successful

- How IT Managers Can Make Innovation Happen: Tips And Techniques For IT Managers To Use In Order To Make Innovation Happen In Their Teams

- Staffing Skills IT Managers Must Have: Tips And Techniques That IT Managers Can Use In Order To Correctly Staff Their Teams

- Secrets Of Effective Leadership For IT Managers: Tips And Techniques That IT Managers Can Use In

Order To Develop Leadership Skills

- IT Manager Career Secrets: Tips And Techniques That IT Managers Can Use In Order To Have A Successful Career

- IT Manager Budgeting Skills: How IT Managers Can Request, Manage, Use, And Track Their Funding

- Secrets Of Managing Budgets: What IT Managers Need To Know In Order To Understand How Their Company Uses Money

Negotiating

- Killer Ways To Prepare For Your Next Negotiation: What You Need To Do BEFORE A Negotiation Starts In Order To Get The Best Possible Outcome

- Getting What You Want In A Negotiation By Learning How To Signal: How To Develop The Skill Of Effective Signaling In A Negotiation In Order To Get The Best Possible Outcome

- Exploring How To Get The Deal That You Want In A Negotiation: How To Develop The Skill Of Exploring What Is Possible In A Negotiation In Order To Reach The Best Possible Deal

- Use The Power Of Arguing To Win Your Next Negotiation: How To Develop The Skill Of Effective Arguing In A Negotiation In Order To Get The Best Possible Outcome

- Learn How To Signal In Your Next Negotiation: How To Develop The Skill Of Effective Signaling In A Negotiation In Order To Get The Best Possible Outcome

- Learn The Skill Of Exploring In A Negotiation: How To Develop The Skill Of Exploring What Is Possible In A Negotiation In Order To Reach The Best Possible Deal

- Learn How To Argue In Your Next Negotiation: How To Develop The Skill Of Effective Arguing In A Negotiation In Order To Get The Best Possible Outcome|

- How To Open Your Next Negotiation: How To Start A Negotiation In Order To Get The Best Possible Outcome

- Preparing For Your Next Negotiation: What You Need To Do BEFORE A Negotiation Starts In Order To Get The Best Possible Deal

- Learn How To Package Trades In Your Next Negotiation

- All Good Things Come To An End: How To Close A Negotiation - How To Develop The Skill Of Closing In Order To Get The Best Possible Outcome From A Negotiation

- Take No Prisoners In Your Next Negotiation: How To Start A Negotiation In Order To Get The Best Possible Outcome

Miscellaneous

- How To Heal A Broken Leg – Fast!: Understanding how to deal with a broken leg in order to start walking again quickly

- How Software Defined Networking (SDN) Is Going To Change Your World Forever: The Revolution In Network Design And How It Affects You

- The Power Of Virtualization: How It Affects Memory, Servers, and Storage: The Revolution In Creating Virtual Devices And How It Affects You

- The Internet-Enabled Successful School District Superintendent: How To Use The Internet To Boost

Parental Involvement In Your Schools

- Power Distribution Unit (PDU) Secrets: What
  Everyone Who Works In A Data Center Needs To
  Know!

- Making The Jump: How To Land Your Dream Job
  When You Get Out Of College!

- How To Use The Internet To Create Successful
  Students And Involved Parents

"Change techniques that will transform a speech into a memorable event

This book has been written with one goal in mind – to show you how you can present a powerful and effective speech. We're going to show you how to use the tools that every speaker has to deliver a great speech!

Let's Make Your Next Speech A Success!

<u>**What You'll Find Inside:**</u>

- **BOUNCING BACK FROM A REALLY BAD SPEECH**

- **LEARN TO READ YOUR NEXT AUDIENCE LIKE A BOOK**

- **HOW TO DEAL WITH SPEAKING ANXIETY WHEN IT COMES**

- **WHAT YOU'VE NEVER BEEN TAUGHT ABOUT BEING A SUCCESSFUL SPEAKER**

Dr. Jim Anderson brings his 25 years of real-world experience to this book. He's delivered speeches at some of the world's largest firms as well as at many conferences. He's going to show you what you need to do in order to make your next speech a success!

Made in the USA
Columbia, SC
31 May 2022

61140480R00052